The Nightingale and the Emperor

A play for children

Alfred Bradley

Adapted from the story by
Hans Christian Andersen

Songs by
Alex Glasgow

Samuel French – London
New York – Sydney – Toronto – Hollywood

THE NIGHTINGALE AND THE EMPEROR

First produced at The Crucible Theatre, Sheffield, on 31st October, 1973.

CHARACTERS

The Emperor of China
The Lord Chancellor
Architect
Housekeeper
Clockmaker
Kay Su, the kitchen maid
Doctor
A Page

SONGS

The music and lyrics are by Alex Glasgow

ACT I

If You Could Climb Inside My Head
Everything In The Emperor's Garden
Grey Bird

ACT II

When The Nightingale Sings
Sprockets And Ratchets
Grey Bird (Reprise)
Who Would Be A Doctor
The Emperor's Dream

See pages 42–51 for the music

AUTHOR'S NOTE

In adapting *The Nightingale* for the stage I have had to make several fundamental changes whilst at the same time attempting to preserve the spirit of Hans Andersen's original story. The time scale has been altered so that the action is continuous and when a composite setting is used the characters can move from the palace to the wood and back without a break. A change of emphasis in the lighting will help to focus attention on each location and the addition of music between the scenes will assist the action to flow smoothly. In Rex Doyle's imaginative first production of the play at The Crucible Theatre in Sheffield the actor who played the Doctor sang the Storyteller's songs and provided most of the musical effects in full view of the audience but there is no reason why the singer should not be played as Hans Andersen himself telling the story from a position outside the main acting area.

The play should not provide many technical problems. The song of the Nightingale can easily be made with a bird warbler which is much easier to cue than a recording of a real nightingale. The clockwork bird needs a little ingenuity but if it sits on a springy perch connected to a clockwork motor it should vibrate easily and a jolt from the Chancellor accompanied by a loud twang offstage will provide the effect when the mechanism is overwound. At one point it is necessary for the real Nightingale to disappear: this may be done by making a false bottom to the cage or by bringing the already empty cage into the palace covered by an embroidered cloth.

In the original story the Nightingale sings directly to the Emperor but of course if this happened on stage we would not know what she was singing or feeling at any particular moment so Kay Su translates the songs into words for us and in a sense embodies the spirit of simplicity and honesty of the Nightingale herself.

Within the play, there are a number of places where characters ask themselves questions and it is important to allow time for the audience to supply the answers so that they realize that they may join in. If the convention is established from the beginning the children will offer advice and encouragement without having to be asked to participate. Any temptation to speak pantomime Chinese or guy the characters should be avoided: the audience will only believe in the people in the story if we believe in them ourselves.

ALFRED BRADLEY

ACT I*

Song: If You Could Climb Inside My Head

Storyteller (*singing*) In the far away time of "once upon a time"
In a once upon a far away land.
If you could climb inside my head,
If you could climb inside my head,
You'd see a story spinning round,
See the pictures, hear the sound.
If you could climb inside my head.
In the far away time of "once upon a time"
In a once upon a far away land.
Since you can't climb inside my head,
Then I'll have to think of something else instead.
We'll put actors in the scenes,
And they'll dramatize the dreams
Since you can't climb inside my head.
In the far away time of "once upon a time"
In a once upon a far away land.

SCENE 1

The Throne Room of the Emperor of China

The Chancellor, a man full of his own importance, comes in

Chancellor This way! Hurry up. Bring the plans in here, the Emperor will be arriving at any moment.

The Architect, a simple hearted young man, comes in after him

Architect I'm coming as quickly as I can. (*He trips as he comes through the doorway and scatters his plans all over the floor*)

Chancellor Oh do hurry up! (*He clears a place on a small table near the throne*) Put them down there. And spread them out so that I can see them properly.

Architect Here we are. (*He spreads the plans*) The plans for the Emperor's new bedroom. I think you'll find them accurate.

Chancellor I'd better peruse them.

---

*N.B. Paragraph 3 on page ii of this Acting Edition regarding photocopying and video-recording should be carefully read.

Architect What?

Chancellor I'd better look them over just in case there are any points which the Emperor doesn't understand. (*He looks at the first plan*) What's this? Six beds! The Emperor has no wives and no children. Why should he need six beds? I've never seen a bedroom like this before, there's a pond in the middle!

Architect Oh dear! (*He peers at the plan*) Oh, I see what's happened, you've got the wrong one. Those are six flower beds and a lily-pond. That's a map of the Emperor's new garden. *This* is the new bedroom. (*He produces another plan from the pile on the table*)

Chancellor Thank goodness. The Emperor wouldn't have thanked you if he had stepped out of bed into a pond each morning. (*He considers the plan for a moment*) What will it be made of?

Architect The walls will be of the purest porcelain.

Chancellor And the floor?

Architect Of the finest marble.

Chancellor And the Emperor's Royal Bathroom?

Architect It will be magnificent.

Chancellor As splendid as all of the other Royal Bathrooms?

Architect Even better! The floor will be of the deepest jade, the walls of clearest crystal and the ceiling of beaten gold.

Chancellor I expect that will do. And what is this other plan?

Architect You will remember that when we finished rebuilding the Royal Kitchen there was a pile of bricks left over: I thought we could use them to build some new rooms above the stables for the grooms and other palace servants.

Chancellor Rooms for the grooms! Whatever next?

Architect Well the new stables are very comfortable for the horses: I just thought it might be an idea to provide rooms so that the servants who look after them could be comfortable as well.

Chancellor (*pushing the plan back to the Architect*) I think it would be most unwise to bother the Emperor with trivialities of that sort. He has far more important things to worry about. Here he comes!

They bow as:

The Emperor comes in

Emperor And what have you for me today, Chancellor?

Chancellor These, Excellency. The finished plans for your new bedroom and the first designs for the new ornamental garden.

Emperor The garden ... let me see what you have in mind. (*He sits on his throne*)

Chancellor Certainly, Excellency. (*He takes the plan from the Architect and hands it to the Emperor*)

Emperor What's this? New rooms for the servants over my Royal Stables! What does this mean?

Architect (*he might as well go through with it*) Just a suggestion, Excellency, there are some bricks left over from the old kitchen and I thought they could be used to make a new quarters for the palace servants.

Emperor And what's wrong with their present quarters?

Architect They're very cold in winter.

Emperor If they're cold, they'd better work harder! I won't agree to it. Pamper servants and you spoil them.

Chancellor Quite right, Excellency. (*He hurriedly changes the plans*) Here are the plans for the garden, Excellency. (*To the Architect*) I told you not to bother the Emperor with things of no importance!

Emperor (*deep in the plans*) This looks very fine. Let me see now, if we clear away the wood on this side of the palace we can have a new courtyard surrounded by six flower beds. What are these?

Architect (*peering at the plan*) They are six bronze towers, Excellency, filled with silver bells. They will tinkle in the breeze to draw visitors' attention to the beauty of the flowers.

Emperor And where is the fountain?

Architect (*pointing to various landmarks on the plan*) Here. The water is pumped from there and splashes from a great height into a pool filled with fish of every colour of the rainbow.

Emperor Good. I like the plan. You can measure up the site and give orders for the woods to be cut down immediately. (*He puts the plan on the seat of his throne*)

Architect If I may make a suggestion, Excellency . . .

Emperor I hope it's better than your last.

Architect Don't you think that it would be better to place the new garden on the other side of the palace?

Emperor But I already have a garden there.

Architect I realize that, Excellency.

Emperor Well?

Architect It's just that it seems a pity to destroy the wood: in Spring it's filled with wild flowers.

Emperor Wild flowers? What place have wild flowers in the grounds of a palace? This is to be a formal garden of great beauty. I don't want to be surrounded by weeds!

Architect Wild flowers in a natural setting can be very beautiful, Excellency.

Emperor If I wanted things to be natural I wouldn't employ an architect. I want this garden to be one of the wonders of the world, do you understand? If you don't, I'll find another architect who does.

Architect (*beaten*) Very well, Excellency.

Emperor And now, Chancellor, let us proceed to the library.

Chancellor Do you wish to read, Excellency?

Emperor Of course not. I want to see how the painters are getting on with the new ceiling. I hope they aren't sleeping on the job.

Chancellor Oh no, Excellency. They *have* to lie on their backs. All the best ceilings are painted that way.

The Chancellor and the Emperor exit

Emperor (*as they go*) Well, I want it finished by the end of this week . . .

Architect (*collecting his plans together*) It's strange that a man with such an eye for beauty doesn't appreciate natural things like woods and wild flowers . . . oh well, perhaps he'll learn in time . . .

The Architect goes out but leaves the garden plan behind on the Emperor's throne

Song: Everything In the Emperor's Garden

Storyteller (*singing*)   Everything in the Emperor's garden
Is the best that money can buy.
Neatly ordered,
Carefully bordered,
Daily watered,
Fertilized.
Prim and proper stand the hedges
And the avenues of beeches
All the lawns arranged and laid out,
Organized.
But down in the woods Mother Nature wears the
    crown.
And the squirrels roam the trees,
And the air fills with the sound
Of the magpies' constant chatter
And the clatter
Of their wings
When the pigeons break from cover
And the nightingale sings.
Shall the blade of the axe
Wreak its havoc on the scene?
Will the Emperor relent
When he hears the woodland's dying screams?

SCENE 2

The same

The Housekeeper enters followed by Kay Su, a young housemaid

Housekeeper Now, Kay Su, come here and I'll tell you what your duties will be. Are you listening carefully?

Kay Su Yes.

Housekeeper This is the Royal Throne Room where the Emperor talks to his advisers.

Kay Su It's very beautiful.

Housekeeper And it's our job to keep it so. Every morning when you have finished your tasks in the kitchen you will take out the ashes from the grate and fill the rush baskets with logs. Have you got that?

Kay Su Yes.

Housekeeper Then you will polish every piece of furniture in this room. The Emperor is likely to fly into a rage if he sees dust anywhere.

Kay Su I'll do my best.

Housekeeper Take this duster. You can start on the throne right now.

Kay Su Thank you. (*She picks up the plan which is lying on the seat of the throne*) What is this?

Housekeeper Let me see. The architect must have left it behind. It looks like the plan for the Emperor's garden.

Kay Su But I thought he had a garden already.

Housekeeper Of course he has. But the Emperor likes to be surrounded with beautiful things so he is always planning something new. They say that the gardens on the far side of the palace are known all over the world, that there are lawns which stretch as far as the eye can see and peacocks who drink from fountains which play sweet music.

Kay Su They say? Haven't you ever seen them?

Housekeeper Of course not. My place is in the kitchen garden. Only the Emperor walks in the palace garden.

Kay Su He must be very lonely.

Housekeeper I daresay. Now come along. Enough talking for one day. I must see that the dining-room is prepared. It's time you were on your way home, child. Don't forget as soon as you arrive tomorrow morning you must polish everything until there isn't the smallest speck of dust to be seen.

The Housekeeper exits

Left on her own. Kay Su talks to the audience

Kay Su Fancy having such a wonderful garden and not being able to share it with anybody . . . (*To the audience*) Have you ever seen a peacock? Are they beautiful? I've never seen one. I haven't heard a musical fountain either. Never mind; every evening on my way home to my mother, I walk through the woods on this side of the palace. They're filled with flowers and they're very beautiful even if there aren't any peacocks . . .

She goes off through the woods singing as she goes

SCENE 3

The same. A week later

The Emperor comes in followed closely by the Chancellor

Emperor What do you think of the new library now that it is finished?

Chancellor Superb, Excellency.

Emperor And the new carpet?

Chancellor Magnificent. Exactly the right colour.

Emperor I'm not sure. Perhaps it's a little too dark.

Chancellor (*anxious to agree*) Now you come to mention it, perhaps it *is* just a little too dark.

Emperor On the other hand, it may be too light . . .

Chancellor That's true. Perhaps it is just a little too light.

Emperor But on the whole . . .

The Chancellor waits to fall in with the Emperor who doesn't finish the sentence

Chancellor Er . . . exactly, it is a wonderful library, Excellency, so dazzling that nobody will be interested in the books.

Emperor All the same it is to be filled with the finest volumes. I will employ a learned scholar to travel across the world in search of the most rare manuscripts.

Chancellor That is an excellent idea. By the way, a book arrived by special messenger today. It is a present from the Shah of Persia.

Emperor Bring it to me.

Chancellor At once, Excellency.

The Chancellor goes to get it

Emperor It is exceedingly kind of the Shah of Persia to send me a present. I expect he has heard about my new library. I wonder what the book will be about? Carpets, I suppose, he's very fond of carpets.

The Chancellor returns with a beautifully-bound, illustrated book

Chancellor Here we are, Excellency. A book which describes the beauties of our city and your palace.

Emperor I can think of no better present. (*He sits on his throne*) Read it to me.

Chancellor Yes, Excellency. (*He clears his throat*) "Travellers who come from all over the world to the City of the Emperor of China are filled with admiration for his fine palace which sits like a jewel on the crown of the hill overlooking the silver river meandering below."

The Emperor, pleased, nods in agreement

"His gardens are the envy of other rulers, his marvellous possessions beyond price—but of all the things in the city, the palace and the gardens, there is nothing like the Nightingale whose song is worth more than anything in all his dominions. Nothing sings more sweetly."

Emperor Stop! What in the world are you saying. The Nightingale. (*He grabs the book from the Chancellor to see for himself*) I have never heard of it. Can there be such a bird in my empire, in my garden even without my having heard of it? One may learn something from books after all. Why has nobody even told me about her?

Chancellor I have never heard her mentioned before. She has certainly never been presented at court.

Emperor It is my Royal Command that she shall come and sing before me this evening. The whole world knows more about her than I know myself.

Chancellor You don't think it might just be an invention of the author? You can't believe everything you read in books, Excellency. Perhaps it is a work of fiction.

Emperor This book was sent to me by the Shah of Persia and therefore it cannot be untrue.

Chancellor But, your Excellency——

Emperor Enough! I wish to hear the Nightingale; she must be here this evening to sing to me at supper. If she hasn't appeared by the time the clock in the North Tower strikes seven, I will have you beaten—and the whole court with you! (*He throws the book to the Chancellor*) I hope I make myself clear.

Chancellor Only too clear, Excellency.

Emperor And you will get a beating each day until the Nightingale is found.

Chancellor Yes, Excellency.

Emperor And stop agreeing with everything I say.

Chancellor Yes, Excellency! I mean, no, Excellency.

Emperor (*going*) Yes, Excellency, yes, Excellency. I could have a better conversation with a ventriloquist's dummy!   ♭

The Emperor exits

Chancellor (*looking hastily at his watch*) Twelve o'clock. If I don't find the Nightingale in the next seven hours I'll be beaten, that's what the Emperor said. (*To the audience*) Do you think he meant it? Yes, so do I! Nobody can have such a difficult life as me. (*He goes to the door and calls*) Architect! If I disagree with the Emperor he flies into a rage; if I agree with him he calls me a dummy. Architect!

The Architect enters carrying a striped pole, ropes and other equipment for surveying the site of the new garden. He trips over the pole and lands in a noisy heap

Architect Who did that?

Chancellor Get up! And put those things down before you do some damage.

Architect I've done myself some damage *already* I think. Did you want me?

Chancellor Yes, but now I come to look at you I don't think you'll be much use. Do you know anything about birds?

Architect I know that they fly.

Chancellor You know that they fly.

Architect Yes. They have wings you know. (*He flaps his arms up and down*) To fly with.

Chancellor (*exasperated*) I have a foot to kick you with! Do you know what the Nightingale looks like?

Architect No, I don't think so, there isn't much demand for them in formal gardens of course. Now peacocks are a different matter. Peacocks are very popular.

Chancellor Yes, I know that. But they don't sing.

Architect No. They don't lay eggs either.

Chancellor Really!

Architect No, peahens lay eggs.

Chancellor Is that all you know about birds?

Architect I'm afraid so. Landscape gardeners spend most of their time frightening birds away. You know, with scarecrows. (*He flings his arms*

out to demonstrate and nearly knocks the Chancellor over) Why do you
want to know about the Nightingale?

Chancellor Because I have to find the bird before seven o'clock tonight. The
Emperor wants me to bring it to him before supper.

Architect Before supper? Is he going to eat it?

Chancellor He wants it to sing for him!

Architect Then he is going to eat it afterwards?

Chancellor No, of course not. It is a thing of beauty.

Architect How do you know if you haven't seen it?

Chancellor Because it says so in a book which the Shah of Persia sent to his
Excellency today.

Architect I see. And what happens if you don't find the Nightingale by
supper time?

Chancellor The Emperor will have me beaten.

Architect That's bad.

Chancellor And the whole court will be beaten as well.

Architect That's *very* bad! I wonder if the Housekeeper can help us? After
all she has lived here longer than anybody.

Chancellor We can try. (*He opens the door and calls*) Housekeeper! She has
worked in the palace all her life but I have never heard her mention the
Nightingale.

The Housekeeper comes in

Housekeeper Did you want me?

Chancellor Yes. What do you know about birds?

Housekeeper A great deal.

Chancellor Go on.

Housekeeper Always pluck them while they're still warm. Clean them well,
stuff them with sage and onions—and always save the giblets for soup.

Chancellor No, no, no. Not chickens! I mean birds that sing.

Housekeeper Oh, like blackbirds, you mean. Well, I usually bake them in a
pie. You should have four and twenty of course—but a couple of dozen
would do.

Chancellor Can't you forget about cooking for a moment?

Housekeeper No, I can't, it's my job; like yours is being pompous.

Chancellor (*about to burst but just containing himself*) What do you know
about the Nightingale?

Housekeeper It isn't mentioned in any recipe book I know.

Chancellor Have you ever seen one?

Housekeeper No.

Chancellor Or heard one sing?

Housekeeper No, never. I haven't time for such things. I spend most of my
time in the kitchen.

Chancellor But when you walk through the fields on your way to work in
the morning?

Housekeeper It's so early that most of the birds aren't awake. Why do you
want to know?

Chancellor Because the Emperor has commanded me to bring the Nightingale to him by seven o'clock tonight.
Housekeeper And if you don't?
Chancellor Then I am to be beaten.
Housekeeper That's bad.
Chancellor And the whole court is to be beaten as well.
Housekeeper That's *very* bad! And you've no idea what the Nightingale looks like or where it lives?
Chancellor No.
Housekeeper I know, the Clockmaker! He is older than anybody else in the palace. Perhaps he knows.
Architect That sounds hopeful.
Housekeeper I'll go and get him.

The Housekeeper goes

Chancellor I'm doomed! I know it. I don't believe the Nightingale exists except in the imagination of the Shah of Persia.

The Housekeeper comes back with the Clockmaker. He is a man obsessed with mechanical gadgets. Old, but bright and cheery

Clockmaker I don't know what you want with me but please hurry. *Tempus fugit.*
Architect Does it?
Chancellor What does he mean?
Architect Time flies.
Clockmaker Yes, and never more than today. Something has gone wrong with the clock in the North Tower; it keeps gaining I'll never get it back to rights if I keep getting interrupted.
Chancellor I have a problem.
Clockmaker *You* have a problem. My life is full of problems and they all go tick, tock.
Chancellor Will you stop talking for a moment and let me speak? I need your help. I have to find a bird by the first stroke of seven tonight.
Clockmaker Why didn't you say so before? That's simple! If everything's adjusted properly you pull the weights, set the pendulum swinging and the bird pops out exactly on the hour.
Chancellor Does it sing?
Clockmaker Not sing exactly.
Chancellor What then?
Clockmaker It says click, click, whirr ... Oh dear, what does it say? I've forgotten. (*To the audience*) What does a cuckoo clock say? What? Cuckoo! That's right. Click, click, whirr, cuckoo! (*He imitates the action of a cuckoo clock poking his head towards the Chancellor*) Then it pops back and shuts the door behind it. There's one in my workshop if you want to see it. Can I go now?
Chancellor No! We don't want a cuckoo clock. We don't want a cuckoo either.

Clockmaker Lots of people do. In Spring they write letters to the newspapers about them. And another thing ...
Chancellor Yes.
Clockmaker They lay their eggs in other birds' nests.
Architect Why do they do that?
Clockmaker Just for a yolk, I suppose.
Chancellor This is no time for yolks. Jokes! The Emperor insists that I present the Nightingale to him tonight.
Clockmaker The Nightingale. I have never heard of it. And what happens if you don't?
Chancellor I will be beaten.
Clockmaker That's bad.
Chancellor And the whole court will be beaten as well.
Clockmaker That's *very* bad! Then there's no time to be lost. On my way back to the Tower I'll ask the Imperial Pastrycooks and the Imperial Plumbers but I don't hold out many hopes. I must go now, if I don't slow the clock down it will be chiming seven before you expect.

The Clockmaker hurries off

Chancellor We're not getting anywhere. (*He turns to the Architect*) Any other ideas?
Architect No. I must go and measure the wood which is to be cut down to make way for the Emperor's new garden. If I meet anybody on the way I'll ask them. Perhaps you'd better talk to the Imperial Musicians, they ought to know how the Nightingale sounds. I'll be back as soon as I can. I hope you're lucky for all our sakes!

The Architect goes off in a muddle of poles and ropes

Chancellor I wish the Emperor had never heard of the Nightingale. I'm certain that nobody else has!

Scene 4

The edge of the Wood

Kay Su is picking flowers. She stops and talks to the audience

Kay Su I'm enjoying working in the Palace. The days are long but the Emperor's Housekeeper is kind to me and I think I'm very lucky to have such a good job. The cook gave me some left-overs yesterday and I took them home to make some soup for my mother who has been ill. She said it was the best soup she had ever tasted: I'm sure that some good food like that will soon make her well again. Last night as I was walking home, at about this time, I heard a bird singing so sweetly. I stopped to listen and then I rememberd that I had heard the same song before when I was walking with my father one summer evening long ago. Can you guess what the bird was? Yes, the Nightingale! After I had listened carefully for some time I found that she was talking to me and I could understand what she was saying.

The Nightingale sings briefly

Good-evening, Nightingale, are you going to sing for us?

The Nightingale sings

What's that? You would like me to sing to you? But my voice isn't beautiful like yours. It's just ordinary . . . very well, I'll try.

Song: Grey Bird

(*Singing*)   Nothing much to look at
Little grey bird, little grey bird,
I'm a grey bird, too,
Grey bird, grey bird,
Little grey bird, I'm a grey bird too.
How I wish that I could sing
How I wish that I had wings
I would fly, fly away and be like you.
Not for me the spring-time blossom
Not for me the trees in autumn
Not for me the summer sky in sunshine
Like the frozen roots of winter
I'm unnoticed and forgotten.
How I wish that I could be like you.

The Nightingale joins in the last few bars but the singers are interrupted by:

The Architect who blunders in. He is still tied up in his measuring equipment

Architect This should be the limit of the lawn, I think. It seems a shame to have to cut down these beautiful trees. They have been growing here since the birth of the Emperor's great-grandfather. Still it's no good arguing with the Emperor. Once he has made his mind up, there's no shifting him. (*He sees Kay Su*) Hello. (*He looks more closely and sees how pretty she is and is overcome with shyness. He shifts from one foot to the other*) Was that you I heard singing just now?

Kay Su Yes. I think it must have been.

Architect Oh . . . why did you stop? I hope I didn't interrupt you.

Kay Su No.

Architect (*after an embarrassed pause*) Oh, good!

Kay Su No, I had come to the end of the song just as you came along.

Architect (*another pause*) Oh I'm glad. (*Hastily*) Not that you had come to the end of the song . . . but glad that I didn't interrupt you . . . what are you doing here?

Kay Su I work in the Emperor's Palace and I'm on my way home. And what are *you* doing?

Architect (*he can't think straight*) Yes.

Kay Su (*laughing*) What are you doing with those ropes and poles?

Architect I'm measuring. (*He begins to set up his equipment and succeeds in tying himself in knots worse than before*)
Kay Su It looks extremely complicated.
Architect It is.
Kay Su What are you measuring?
Architect The distance from the edge of the wood to the palace. The Emperor wants a new garden, and he has decided that it should be placed here.
Kay Su But won't the trees be in the way?
Architect They would be if they were left; the Emperor is going to have them cut down.
Kay Su All of them?
Architect All of them.
Kay Su Oh, no! But that's terrible. (*It looks as if she might cry*)
Architect I'm very sorry about it too. But there are other woods not so far away, you can still walk there.
Kay Su You don't understand. If you cut down this wood you will disturb the Nightingale!
Architect That can't be helped. I'm afraid. (*He realizes what she has said*) The Nightingale! Did you say the Nightingale?
Kay Su Yes.
Architect Where is she?
Kay Su She lives here in the shade of the wood.
Architect But how do you know that?
Kay Su Because I hear her singing, of course.
Architect (*hardly able to believe his ears*) You hear her singing? (*To the audience*) She must have made a mistake. Do you think it really is the Nightingale? In this wood? That's wonderful news! Little maid, what is your name?
Kay Su Kay Su.
Architect Kay Su. Please come with me at once to the Lord Chancellor. He needs your help badly.
Kay Su Whatever could a poor girl like me do for the mighty Lord Chancellor?
Architect Come with me and find out. I promise that you won't regret it.
Kay Su All right. But I can't stay long. I told my mother that I would not be late home and I don't want her to worry about me.
Architect Hurry please, we haven't much time . . .

SCENE 5

The Palace

The Chancellor is arguing with the Clockmaker

Chancellor Time, time, time. That's all you talk about!
Clockmaker What else? It's my living. The clock has to be exactly right.

Chancellor Can't you slow it down? Or even stop it—then seven o'clock would never come?

Clockmaker Listen, I'm sorry for you. I understand how desperate you must be but it's more than my life's worth to alter the time deliberately. Besides I have some pride in my profession. You've still got an hour to find the Nightingale.

Chancellor An hour! Oh, why doesn't anybody help me. Why am I surrounded by fools.

The Housekeeper hurries in

Housekeeper What's going on? It sounds so stormy, I'm surprised the milk hasn't turned sour.

Chancellor (*petulantly*) It's his fault. He could change the time if he wanted but he won't. Remember that when we're being beaten.

The Architect comes in, still carrying his paraphernalia

Architect Chancellor, your worries are at an end.

Chancellor Here's another of them! Now, what is it?

Architect I've been measuring the woods to mark out the exact place for the Emperor's new garden.

Chancellor I know that.

Architect And who do you think I met there?

Chancellor (*with exaggerated patience*) The three bears?

Architect No. A little maid from the kitchen. Come in, Kay Su!

Kay Su comes in

Housekeeper Whatever are you doing here, child, you set off for home an hour ago. Why are you so late?

Kay Su I was on my way home but I stopped to talk to the Nightingale.

Chancellor You stopped to talk to what?

Kay Su The Nightingale.

Chancellor I can't believe it!

Kay Su It's true. I talked to her last night as well.

Chancellor This is wonderful news! You have come just in time. The Emperor has commanded that the Nightingale should appear before him this evening.

Kay Su Yes?

Chancellor If you will conduct us to her, I will see that you are promoted. I may even allow you to peep at the Emperor himself.

Kay Su Will you promise not to hurt her?

Chancellor Of course.

Kay Su Very well. I will take you to her. Have you a box to put her in?

Chancellor I have a small wicker basket. (*He produces it*) Don't worry, she won't be locked in, there is no lid you see. Do you remember the way?

Kay Su Yes. (*She moves towards the wood*)

Housekeeper I'll come with you. I'd like to hear a Nightingale.

Architect And I'll come too.

Kay Su, the Chancellor, the Housekeeper and the Architect go

Clockmaker I won't. If nobody wants me I'll go back to the clock tower. (*He looks at his pocket watch*) It's a quarter past six, you haven't got long ... tick, tock, tick, tock ...

SCENE 6

Towards the Wood

The Chancellor, Kay Su, the Housekeeper and the Architect are walking towards the wood

Kay Su This way, it isn't very far.

A frog croaks nearby

Chancellor Ah! Now I hear her.
Kay Su Who?
Chancellor Listen!

The frog croaks again

The Nightingale! (*To the audience*) That is the Nightingale, isn't it? No? What is it then? A frog. Of course it is, I knew all the time!

A cow begins to moo

Chancellor What a beautiful voice. That's the Nightingale, isn't it? No? What is it then? A cow. Of course it is, anybody would know that!
Kay Su We won't be long now: this is where she lives. Listen!

They all wait in silence and are rewarded by a song from the Nightingale

Chancellor (*looking up to where the Nightingale sits*) Is it possible that such a little grey bird can make such a song? Perhaps she has changed colour at the sight of somebody as important as me.
Kay Su Little Nightingale. Our precious Emperor wishes you to sing something for him.

A short song

Chancellor What does she say?
Kay Su She says she will be pleased to sing for the Emperor.
Housekeeper It sounds like glass bells. And look at her little throat how it moves!
Architect She will have great success at court.
Chancellor Undoubtedly. Most excellent Nightingale, I have the honour to invite you to a court festival which is to take place this evening when his Imperial Majesty will doubtless be enchanted with your delightful song.

The Nightingale sings

Chancellor What does she say?

Kay Su She was under the impression that you were the Emperor.
Chancellor (*preening*) That's understandable, I suppose.
Kay Su She also says that her song would sound far better among the green
  trees, but she will come to the Palace if the Emperor wishes it.
Chancellor Then ask her to step into her basket and we'll all make haste
  back to the Palace.
Kay Su Sweet Nightingale, will you step into this basket? I promise that no
  harm will befall you. (*She lifts the basket up to the tree and the Nightingale
  disappears into it*)
Chancellor That's good. Right then off we go to the Palace. (*He turns to
  Kay Su*) And for the help you have given, I will arrange for you to listen to
  the proceedings from behind the door to the Throne Room. Now you
  couldn't have fairer than that ...

SCENE 7

The Palace

Clockmaker It's three minutes to seven by my watch. I'd like to help the
  Chancellor, he's a pompous old fool, but he has never done me any harm.
  But it's more than my job's worth to go round the Palace stopping the
  clocks. Besides, the Emperor isn't stupid, he'd soon catch on. No, I think
  we have to face it, we're all in for a beating. I think I'll get ready for it. (*He
  stuffs a thick book down the back of his trousers. He wriggles about trying
  to get comfortable*)

The Emperor appears

Emperor Is there something wrong, Clockmaker?
Clockmaker No! Er, I was just practising a new dance step.
Emperor That could be dangerous at your age. Have you mended the clock
  in the North Tower yet?
Clockmaker Yes, Excellency. It is absolutely correct.
Emperor And the time now is?

The clock strikes

Clockmaker Seven, exactly. (*He checks his watch*) Good, very good. (*Back-
  ing away to avoid the beating which now seems a certainty*) I'd better get
  back to the clocktower ... make sure it's fully wound.

The Clockmaker scurries off

Emperor Where is the Chancellor? And more important, where is the
  Nightingale?

The Chancellor followed by the Architect puffs into the room

Chancellor Excellency, forgive my lateness, but I bring good news. Sensa-
  tional news.
Emperor What is it?

Chancellor The Nightingale has been found!

Emperor That is good news indeed. And who found her?

Chancellor (*boasting*) I did, your Excellency! (*Putting on a false modesty*) It wasn't difficult really.

Emperor Splendid. We will see her immediately.

The Chancellor claps his hands

A Page brings the Nightingale who is now perched in a small golden cage resting on a red velvet cushion. The Page places the cage on a small table next to the Emperor's chair and exits

One can hardly believe that such an ordinary looking bird can enchant the ears of wise men all over the world.

Chancellor Are you ready to hear her, Excellency?

The Emperor nods

Nightingale, the Emperor commands you to sing for him!

The Nightingale is silent. The courtiers look at each other in dismay

Emperor Well?

Chancellor (*flustered*) I don't know what can be the matter, Excellency. (*He tries again*) Nightingale! You are bidden to sing for the Emperor!

Still no song

Emperor Is this some jest?

Chancellor No. I don't understand it. She sang before.

Emperor You say she sang before? Then why won't she sing now? Did you really find her yourself?

Chancellor Yes, I did. (*To the audience*) Didn't I? Oh yes I did!

Emperor (*when things are quiet again*) If you didn't, who did? (*To the audience*) Kay Su? Who is Kay Su?

Architect Excuse me, Excellency ... With your permission ...

He moves to the door and comes back with Kay Su who curtsies before the Emperor

Emperor And who is this?

Architect This is Kay Su, the new maid in the kitchen. It is she who *really* found the Nightingale.

Emperor Is this true?

Chancellor (*looking sheepish*) Well, perhaps she did have *something* to do with it.

Architect Maybe *she* can persuade her to sing.

The Emperor beckons Kay Su towards the Nightingale

Kay Su (*gently*) Little Nightingale, the Emperor has been told about your voice and would like to hear it for himself. Will you please sing for him?

The Nightingale sings. The court is delighted and the Emperor in particular, moved to tears

Emperor That is the most beautiful song I have ever heard. (*To Kay Su*) Will you please tell the Nightingale that she will henceforward be called the Emperor's Nightingale and shall be given a golden cage set with precious stones?

The Nightingale answers

Kay Su The Nightingale thanks your Excellency but says that she has seen tears in the eyes of the Emperor and that is the greatest reward she could have.

Emperor Little maid, you shall be the Nightingale's keeper.

The Chancellor looks put out

From now on, it will be your job to look after her and to tell me what she says. She will be secured to the cage by a long silken thread so that she is free to fly. (*To the Chancellor*) See that the maid is given suitable attire.

The Chancellor doesn't like Kay Su's sudden move up into the world of the court but has to make the best of it

Chancellor Yes, Excellency. (*He claps his hands*)

The Page enters and dresses Kay Su in a golden kimono

The Nightingale sings

Emperor What does she say?

Kay Su The Nightingale thanks your Excellency for the honour you have bestowed upon her and also thanks you for having allowed her to live in the woods on your estate for so long. She says that you are a wise Emperor to have allowed the beauties of nature to remain unspoiled.

Emperor (*embarrassed*) Yes ... thank you. Architect!

Architect Excellency?

Emperor Erm ... I've changed my mind about the wood. I think we'll have the new garden on the other side of the Palace after all.

Architect (*delighted*) A wise emperor indeed!

The Emperor goes off followed by Kay Su with the Nightingale

Now I can get to work with a good heart.

The Architect goes off with the Housekeeper, leaving the Chancellor alone

Chancellor (*brooding*) I don't like the way things are going ... I don't like the way things are going at all. I daresay the Nightingale sings sweetly enough—if you like that sort of thing—but there must be other birds that sing as well. (*To the audience*) And did you notice how that little kitchen maid was promoted on the spot just because she could understand what the bird was saying? She has taken my place at the Emperor's side already and probably thinks she will become even more important. I don't like her, do you? Do you? Well, she'd better watch out. If I get my way it won't be long before she is out of those fine robes and back in the kitchen for good!

CURTAIN

ACT II

Song: When The Nightingale Sings

Storyteller (*singing*)

> Have you noticed what has happened
> Since the first time I appeared?
> The story in my head
> Is tumbling out so you can hear.
> The Nightingale was singing
> In my little head alone,
> Now it's singing in your head
> You can hear its silver tone.

(*Chorus*)

> And when the Nightingale sings
> I know that everybody sings.
> And when everybody sings
> I know what happiness it brings
> So sing, little Nightingale,
> Sing, little Nightingale,
>
> Sing, little Nightingale,
> Sing.
>
> And the story still spinning in my head
> Has only half been told.
> The actors have the details
> Which they'll very soon unfold.
> The Architect, the Chancellor,
> The Emperor and all
> Are standing in the wings
> Where they're waiting for the call.

(*Chorus*)

> And when the Nightingale sings
> I know that everybody sings.
> And when everybody sings
> I know what happiness it brings
> So sing, little Nightingale,
> Sing, little Nightingale,
> Sing, little Nightingale,
> Sing.

SCENE 1

The Throne Room

The Housekeeper chats to the audience

Housekeeper Do you know, it's three months since the Nightingale arrived at the palace and I've never seen the Emperor so happy. Kay Su seems to like her new job as keeper of the Imperial Nightingale and is now allowed to walk in the Emperor's garden. But she is a modest girl and she hasn't let her new position go to her head. Every evening she comes to the kitchen and tells me what the Nightingale has been singing. I haven't much time for singing-birds really, but I don't tell her that. And there's no doubt the Nightingale *has* got a lovely voice.

The Architect comes in carrying a package

Architect Who are you talking to?

Housekeeper Eh? Oh, just thinking aloud! I do that now and then. What's that?

Architect A package addressed to the Emperor. Just arrived.

Housekeeper It's an interesting looking parcel.

Architect Yes, I can't think what it can be.

Housekeeper What does it say on the label.

Architect "Nightingale" that's all. Perhaps it's another book about our far-famed bird. But it's a funny shape for a book.

Housekeeper I wish it was a new recipe book. Now, that would be useful.

The Housekeeper goes off, bumping into the Chancellor as he comes in

Chancellor (*short tempered*) Watch where you're going! Now, Architect, what have you got there?

Architect I think it's another book.

Chancellor Let's hope this one doesn't tell us about the beauty of the Dodo! (*He takes the parcel*) It doesn't feel like a book. (*He shakes it*) It doesn't sound like a book.

The Emperor comes in accompanied by Kay Su who is carrying the Nightingale's cage

Emperor (*genially*) Good-morning!

Chancellor Good-morning, Excellency!

Architect Good morning, Excellency. Hello, Kay Su.

Kay Su Hello.

Chancellor Excellency——

Emperor One moment, Chancellor. Kay Su, will you place the Nightingale near the window where she can see the woods?

Kay Su Yes, Excellency.

Emperor And then you can come and sit here beside me. Now, Chancellor.

Chancellor This parcel has just arrived for you. It is marked "Nightingale" and nothing more. We were wondering what was inside it.

Emperor There's a very good way to find out.
Chancellor Yes, Excellency? How?
Emperor By opening it.
Chancellor What a very good idea. I love opening parcels.

He unties the string and uncovers a clockwork Nightingale covered with precious stones. It is larger than the real Nightingale and is on a perch which sits on an ornate plinth which conceals the mechanism

It is a Nightingale, Excellency. (*He can't resist a dig at Kay Su*) And a bird of fitting appearance for the court of an Emperor. It has a band round its neck which bears an inscription.
Emperor What does it say?
Chancellor "The gift of the Emperor of Japan." Isn't it beautiful.
Architect Yes. But it can't sing like the real Nightingale.
Chancellor Just a moment, there's a key here. I'll wind it up and we'll see what happens. (*He winds the mechanism and the bird begins to sing. It makes a pleasant enough sound but the rhythm is repetitive and predictable*)
Emperor It is very kind of the Emperor of Japan to send me such a splendid gift.
Chancellor The real Nightingale sings very well, of course, but in some ways this is even better for one can remember the tune more easily.

The bird stops

Emperor Is anything wrong?
Chancellor No, Excellency. It just needs winding up again. (*He winds it up and it sings the song again*)
Emperor See how the jewels sparkle as the bird sings! It is a pity that it sings only one song but it is a pretty song all the same. Don't you think so, Kay Su?
Kay Su It is very beautiful and must have been made with great care. But there is nothing to compare with the song of the real Nightingale.
Chancellor Perhaps the mechanical bird and the Nightingale could sing together.
Emperor A duet? What a good idea. Kay Su, bring the Imperial Nightingale closer and we will hear the two birds sing in harmony.

Kay Su hesitates

What is the matter, child?
Kay Su I'm not sure that the sounds will go well together, Excellency.
Emperor Let us judge that when we have heard them.

Kay Su brings the Nightingale's cage closer to the mechanical bird

Is the mechanism wound up, Chancellor?
Chancellor Yes, Excellency.
Emperor Then we will begin.

The mechanical bird sings but the Nightingale is silent

Chancellor What is the matter? Doesn't the Nightingale know what is required of her?

Kay Su I'm not sure. Sweet Nightingale, his Excellency would like you to sing a duet with the new nightingale from Japan. (*Silence, she looks into the cage*) Oh!

Emperor What is it?

Kay Su She isn't there!

Emperor Not there?

Kay Su She seems to have flown away.

Architect But I didn't see her go.

Emperor Nor I.

Kay Su Her cage was by the open window. She must have decided to fly away while we were listening to the nightingale from Japan. (*She hurries to the window and calls*) Nightingale!

There is no reply

Emperor We can soon bring her back. All we have to do is pull the silken thread gently and she will return to us.

Kay Su No, Excellency.

Emperor What do you mean?

Kay Su There *is* no silken thread.

Emperor But there must be. I ordered it so.

Kay Su I know. But I could not bring myself to tie her even by a silken thread. I promised that she should remain free and the thread would have bound her and made her unhappy.

Emperor And now, instead, I am unhappy. I appointed you to look after the Nightingale and you have failed me. I told you to secure her and you have disobeyed me.

Kay Su I'm sure she will come back. I will go to the woods and call her. (*She looks at the Emperor's stern face*) I'm sorry.

Emperor Your presence here reminds me of the treasure I have lost. I never wish to set eyes on you again—unless you bring the Nightingale with you.

Kay Su is desolate. She is about to speak but thinks better of it and runs from the palace

Chancellor (*hardly able to conceal his pleasure at the way things have gone*) Even if the little grey Nightingale doesn't come back, Excellency, you still have the beautiful Japanese Nightingale.

He sets it singing and nods his head cheerfully in time with the music. The Emperor sits staring into space

Song: Sprockets and Ratchets

Storyteller (*singing*)   Take some sprockets and ratchets
And springs and some gadgets
Some spindles and handles and screws.
It may seem absurd
But you can make a bird

Which will sing all the time if you choose.
It will sing in the morning,
And sing in the evening,
It will warble at midnight or noon,
At the turn of a key
It will whistle with glee
But always the very same tune.
Always the very same tune.
But should you wish to hear a nightingale
Pouring forth its silver to the sky
You must wait very still
You must wait for the thrill
And you'll hear it if you're patient by and by.

SCENE 2

Another part of the Palace

Housekeeper Kay Su came to me as soon as she had left the throne room: she told me all that had happened and how angry the Emperor had been. (*To the audience*) I don't think it was her fault, do you? Of course, she did disobey an order, but I think she did it for the best of reasons. She couldn't know that the Nightingale would decide to fly away like that, could she? Now that she is no longer keeper of the Imperial Nightingale she has come back to work with me. And although I'm sorry about what has happened, I'm very glad to have her to help me again. She has been here for a week and it's made such a difference.

Kay Su comes in. She is dressed as a kitchen maid again

Housekeeper Now, child?
Kay Su It's nearly six o'clock. Have you any more tasks for me today?
Housekeeper Have you mixed the dough for tomorrow's bread?
Kay Su Yes.
Housekeeper And made all the beds?
Kay Su Yes.
Housekeeper And cleaned the grates?
Kay Su Yes.
Housekeeper That seems to be all.
Kay Su I haven't dusted the furniture in the Imperial throne room. I keep putting it off.
Housekeeper But I thought that was one of the tasks you enjoyed most.
Kay Su It was. Now it only reminds me of the Emperor. I remember how he looked at me when the Nightingale flew away. I'm being silly I suppose. I'll do it tomorrow.
Housekeeper Very well. Now it will soon be dark; the nights are beginning to draw in, I think you ought to set off home. I suppose you haven't heard anything of the Nightingale?

Kay Su Not a sound since that day. Each night as I go through the woods I call to her but she doesn't answer. The Emperor doesn't need her now that he has the clockwork bird which will sing to anybody's bidding as often as you please, but *I* miss her so much.
Housekeeper You go on searching, child. Maybe she will hear you one day.
Kay Su I will, good-night.

Kay Su goes

Housekeeper I'm afraid it isn't very likely that she'll find the Nightingale again. (*To the audience*) Do you think she will? Well, I hope you're right. Even if it's only in her dreams . . .

SCENE 3

The Wood

Kay Su is walking in the wood

Kay Su It was about here that I first heard her, but I can't be sure because most of the flowers have faded with the coming of Autumn and one tree looks very like another. (*She calls*) Nightingale! Nightingale, please answer me. Even though the Emperor may not need you any more, I do. Nightingale! Oh, well, if you won't sing to me I'll sing to you. (*She sings a sad version of "Grey Bird"*)

Song: Grey Bird (Reprise)

> Nothing much to look at.
> Little grey bird, little grey bird,
> I'm a grey bird too,
> Grey bird, grey bird,
> Little grey bird, I'm a grey bird too.
> How I wish that I could sing
> How I wish that I had wings
> I would fly, fly away and be like you.
> Not for me the spring-time blossom
> Not for me the trees in autumn
> Not for me the summer sky in sunshine
> Like the frozen roots of winter
> I'm unnoticed and forgotten.
> How I wish that I could be like you.

The Architect comes blundering into the wood carrying a knot of ropes and poles

Architect Oh, hello, I always seem to interrupt your singing. I'm very sorry. It isn't often that people sing nowadays and you can't go walking round on tiptoe just in case.
Kay Su That's all right. But I wasn't singing because I was happy.

Architect What *were* you singing about?

Kay Su I was singing to the Nightingale, hoping that she would come back. Oh, I wish she would!

Architect You're not the only one. The Emperor seemed so much more contented when she was in the Palace. A changed man you might say. In fact he seemed to enjoy life more than he ever has before. It gave me the courage to tackle him on a subject that's very important to me.

Kay Su What was that?

Architect It's a long story but in a corner of the courtyard there is a pile of bricks and stones which nobody has any use for. They were left over when the kitchen was rebuilt and I wanted to use them to build new rooms for the Emperor's servants.

Kay Su That seems a good idea. The bricks aren't much use just lying in a heap.

Architect Exactly, but the Emperor wouldn't hear of it. I had given up hope but then he changed—became so much better tempered that I thought I would try again. But when I approached him the morning after the Nightingale left us he flew into a temper and not only refused to consider the idea but said he had changed his mind about the other plan as well.

Kay Su What plan was that?

Architect The plan for the garden. It is to be made at *this* side of the Palace after all.

Kay Su Oh no!

Architect He refused to listen to my arguments for keeping the wood, saying that now there was no Nightingale there was no need to preserve the trees.

Kay Su But the wood is beautiful. Are you sure he won't change his mind?

Architect Not a hope. That's why I'm here, to measure up the site and mark the trees which have to be cut down. It's very depressing.

Kay Su What about all of your other plans, are they going well?

Architect I suppose so, but the Emperor shows no great pleasure in them. I presented him with the preliminary plans for the new Imperial Ballroom yesterday; he nodded at all of my suggestions, but I have never seen a man less likely to dance.

Kay Su I'm sorry, it seems that I am largely to blame. It was my fault that the Nightingale was free to fly away. But I'll go on searching in the hope that one day her song may brighten the Emperor's life again. Goodbye, I must go home now.

Architect Goodbye, little Kay Su.

She goes off and we hear her still calling the Nightingale in the distance

I suppose I had better get on with the measuring: I've never taken so long over a job in my life before. That's because my heart isn't in it I suppose . . .

SCENE 4

The Throne Room

The clock chimes eight

Kay Su comes in

Kay Su I've emptied the ashes and filled the log baskets, there's just the furniture to be polished. (*She begins to work*)

The Chancellor comes in and sees Kay Su

Chancellor (*putting on a very superior air*) Let me see, it's Kay Su, the poor little kitchen maid, isn't it?

Kay Su You know very well it is.

Chancellor So you have gone back to your old occupation! Once a skivvy always a skivvy, I say. I never felt that you were the right sort of person to have at court. What does the Emperor see in her I would ask myself—and I could never think of a reply.

Kay Su That is surprising: it isn't often that you are lost for words.

Chancellor Oh, very droll. I suppose you know that the Emperor has seen fit to bestow on the Japanese nightingale the title of "High Imperial After Dinner Singer".

Kay Su That is a great honour for her.

Chancellor And an even greater honour for me. After your bird had flown away, the Emperor made me "Keeper of the High Imperial After Dinner Singer". And unlike your ungrateful Nightingale, mine sings for him every day.

Kay Su And does he never tire of her song?

Chancellor Of course not. Artists have come from many countries to paint pictures of her and musicians to listen to her song. And they say that it is superior to the living Nightingale for not only does it observe a pattern in its singing which everybody can follow, but it sparkles with jewels— particularly now that the Emperor has had a new collar of emeralds placed round its neck.

Kay Su I am pleased that the Japanese Nightingale makes the Emperor happy.

Chancellor The other bird was so unpredictable—and so very, *very* grey.

Kay Su (*near to tears*) Is there anything else you wish to say to me, Chancellor?

Chancellor (*mocking her voice*) Is there anything else you wish to say to me, Chancellor? Yes there is. I was closer to the Emperor than anybody else until you came along. Now I am at his right hand again and you are back where you came from. You can be sure that you will never get another chance to usurp my position.

Kay Su But you've got the wrong idea! I never tried to take your place. It was the Emperor who decided to make me "Keeper of the Imperial Nightingale".

Chancellor Yes, and it was the Emperor who banished you. And he is so contented with the new Nightingale that he would not have you back even if your precious little bird decided to condescend to return to the Palace. Yesterday he solemnly declared that the Nightingale was henceforth banished from his dominions.

Kay Su I don't know why you get so much pleasure from hurting me like this. It was you who asked me to bring the Nightingale here: I wish I had kept the secret of her singing to myself. I have finished my task so I will bid you good-day, Chancellor!

Chancellor (*delighted that he has needled her*) Good-day! I'd hurry if I were you, the Emperor won't take kindly to your presence in his throne room.

Kay Su goes

That's the last we'll see of her for some time I expect. (*To the audience*) I'm glad to see the back of her, aren't you? Well, I am! I'm very glad! Ha! ha! ha! (*He jumps for joy*) Ha! ha! ha!

The Emperor comes in suddenly

Emperor What ever is going on? Is this the way you behave in my throne room when I am not present?

Chancellor No, Excellency.

Emperor Yes, Excellency! I haven't slept for three nights. I have a headache and it is not helped by the noisy cavorting of simpletons.

Chancellor A headache? (*Very solicitous*) Perhaps you would like to rest, Excellency?

Emperor Rest! I've been trying to rest. But the same thoughts keep going round and round in my head.

Chancellor Perhaps it would take your mind off things if you were to look at the plans for your new Imperial Bathing Pool.

Emperor If you don't want me to go off the deep end you'll stop burbling and call for my doctor.

Chancellor Of course, Excellency. (*He crosses to the door*) Call the Imperial Doctor!

Voice (*off*) Call the Imperial Doctor!

Emperor And do it quietly!

Chancellor And do it quietly!

Voice (*off*) And do it quietly!

The Emperor's expression suggests that he can't take much more of this but before he can explode:

The Doctor arrives

Doctor (*bright and hearty*) Now, Excellency, what seems to be wrong?

Emperor Nothings *seems* to be wrong. It *is* wrong. My head aches and it won't stop.

Doctor (*breezily*) That shouldn't be difficult to cure.

Emperor I wish you would not be so hearty! Just tell me what is wrong and what I need to do to stop the sledgehammer that is pounding my brain.

Doctor Just one moment. (*He takes his pulse*) That seems to be all right.
Emperor What now?
Doctor You took the pink pills which I prescribed yesterday?
Emperor Yes. And the yellow ones which you prescribed the day before.
Doctor And they had no effect?
Emperor Do they look as if they had?
Doctor One moment: (*He pulls out his stethoscope and listens to the Emperor's heart*) Yes. Yes. Yes. No. (*He shakes his head solemnly*)
Emperor Well?
Doctor I want you to take this prescription to the Imperial Dispenser. (*He hands a prescription to the Chancellor*) He will make up some special Imperial Medicine. The Emperor is to take an Imperial measure three times a day. (*To the Emperor*) I will call again tomorrow, Excellency.

He goes

Emperor What does the prescription say?
Chancellor How can I tell? It's in Greek.
Emperor It can't be. Doctors always write in Latin.
Chancellor It's *all* Greek to me.
Emperor Just read what it says.
Chancellor Well the doctor seems to have diagnosed your complaint. It says here "Nature of Complaint" and then the Doctor has written "*Nescio*". That's what you are suffering from. "*Nescio*".
Emperor Nature of complaint *Nescio*. That's Latin for I don't know! (*He rises from his throne angrily*) That charlatan is doping me with pills and powders and potions and he doesn't know what is the matter with me!
Chancellor Perhaps if you took things calmly for a while, Excellency . . . the events of the last few days have been a strain. Sit down and rest and forget about your problems. Maybe you would like to listen to the High Imperial After Dinner Singer?
Emperor The what?
Chancellor The clockwork Nightingale.
Emperor Oh, very well. (*He sits*) Let us hear its song once again.
Chancellor (*pleased*) Yes, Excellency. I think that's a very good idea. (*He rushes to get it*) There's nothing like music for soothing a savage headache. *This* Nightingale will never desert you, of that you may be quite sure. This one will sing as often as you wish for ever and ever. (*As he burbles on he continues to wind the mechanism, suddenly there is a bang as the spring breaks. The bird flutters and chirps at high speed for a moment and then runs down to an awful silence*)
Emperor And now what have you done?
Chancellor (*looking sadly at the remains*) I'm afraid . . . it appears to have broken!
Emperor (*heavily*) And who appears to have broken it?
Chancellor I do, Excellency.
Emperor Well, don't just stand there!
Chancellor No, Excellency. (*He rushes to the door*)
Emperor Where are you going?

Chancellor I don't know. You told me not to stand there so I thought I'd go.
Emperor Come here. (*Patiently*) Go to the Imperial Clockmaker and see if he can do anything.
Chancellor Yes, Excellency. (*He rushes in the other direction*)
Emperor And take the clockwork bird with you.
Chancellor Yes, Excellency!

The Chancellor rushes back, picks up the bird and hurries off

Emperor I'm surrounded by frauds and fools. No wonder I don't feel well.

The Emperor goes off

SCENE 5

The Wood

The Doctor is on his way home when he hears somebody whistling

Doctor What's that? (*To the audience*) Did you hear something? What was it? Could it have been the famous Nightingale? Will you let me know if you see anybody? Thank you. Where? Over there? I can't see anybody . . .

The Architect comes in behind him

Architect Hello!
Doctor What! Oh, it's you. Isn't it late to be working?
Architect Yes, but it's a job I'm not very enthusiastic about so I'm not getting on very quickly. Are you on your way home?
Doctor Yes.
Architect And how is the Emperor today?
Doctor As well as can be expected.
Architect I suppose that depends on what you expect.
Doctor (*turning to him suddenly*) Are you an honest man?
Architect I think so.
Doctor Then I'll tell you something. I've nobody else to confide in.
Architect Go on.
Doctor I've examined the Emperor thoroughly and there's nothing wrong with him.
Architect But he says he's ill. He certainly looks unhappy.
Doctor Of course he does but my diagnosis is that he is just bored. He would deny it, of course, but I think he misses the Nightingale. He would like her to come back and he won't admit it. Like all important men, he is lonely and needs companionship.
Architect Don't forget he banished her from his kingdom. It's a bit difficult to change that. I mean it's easy to say "I banish you". It's not so easy to say "I unbanish you".
Doctor It's a pity that such a good ruler has to be so stubborn. It does

nobody any good. If he goes on like this he'll think himself into a real illness.

Architect I thought that the clockwork Nightingale made him happy.

Doctor It did for a while. But have you heard that tune? It's amusing the first time or two but it goes on and on like an everlasting hurdy-gurdy. And he can't talk to it: you can't have a conversation with something you wind up. No, I'm certain that what he wants is the real Nightingale for company.

Architect Then why don't you tell him so?

Doctor And get my head bitten off?

Architect A moment ago you asked me if I was an honest man. As an honest Doctor it's your job to tell the Emperor the truth.

Doctor Even if he doesn't want to hear it?

Architect Particularly if he doesn't want to hear it.

Doctor Do you realize what you're asking? I'll lose my job for sure.

Architect It can't be much of a job if you can't tell your patients the truth.

Doctor (*to the audience*) Shall I tell him the truth? Even if it means that I'll lose my job? You're right, I must tell him. I'll do it tomorrow. Thank you for helping me to make up my mind. Good-night!

The Doctor goes

Architect Good-night. It's easy giving other people advice, isn't it? I wish I had the courage to tell the Emperor that I'm not going to destroy this wood!

Song: Who Would Be A Doctor

Storyteller (*singing*) Who would be a doctor
For a ruler of his kind?
He feels so sick but doesn't know
The trouble's in his mind.

Dearie me, dearie me,
Oh, dear, dearie me!
He feels so sick but doesn't know
The trouble's in his mind.

He'll find no cure in tablets
In potions or in pills
Everybody knows but him
The medicine for his ills.

Dearie me, dearie me,
Oh, dear, dearie me!
Everybody knows but him
The medicine for his ills.

But if our Doctor tells him
It may land him in a mess

He might be banished from the kingdom
Or something even worse!

Dearie me, dearie me,
Oh, dear, dearie me!
He might be banished from the kingdom
Or something even worse!

He could even have his head chopped off
Or be strung up from a tree
I can't tell you what might happen
You'll just have to wait and see.

Dearie me, dearie me,
Oh, dear, dearie me!
I can't tell you what might happen
You'll just have to wait and see.

Scene 6

The Throne Room

The Emperor is seated on his throne but has a footstool and is to all intents and purposes in bed

The Chancellor comes in

Emperor (*wearily*) Well, Chancellor, what are the plans for today?
Chancellor Good news, Excellency!
Emperor Go on.
Chancellor The Imperial Clockmaker awaits, your Excellency.
Emperor Old tick-tock. What does he want?
Chancellor He has examined the High Imperial After Dinner Singer.
Emperor What?
Chancellor The clockwork Nightingale. He wishes to bring it to you.
Emperor All right. It may take my mind off other problems. Let him come in.
Chancellor (*clapping his hands*) Let the Imperial Clockmaker present himself to the Emperor!
Voice (*off*) Let the Imperial Clockmaker present himself to the Emperor!
Emperor (*as the shouting sets his nerves jangling*) I don't know why people can't just come in without all that noise. (*Shouting*) Doesn't anybody care about my headache?

The Clockmaker comes in bearing the clockwork Nightingale which has been mended. He carries it proudly to the Emperor

Well, clockmaker, have you had any success?
Clockmaker It hasn't been easy. A most intricate mechanism. The balance

wheel was upset when the spring snapped causing the main bearing to rotate in a somewhat eccentric manner. Now of course that means that when the cogs intermesh——

Emperor Enough! I don't want a lecture on mechanics. Does the bird sing as well as before?

Clockmaker It sings, Excellency, certainly.

Emperor But not as well as before ...

Clockmaker I wouldn't say that, but it sings differently.

Emperor Let us hear for ourselves.

The Clockmaker bows and hands the clockwork bird to the Chancellor who is about to wind it up when he is stopped by the Emperor

No Chancellor, I am sure you are good at many things, but I think you had better let the Clockmaker wind the bird up this time.

The Chancellor, obviously put out, hands the clockwork bird back to the Clockmaker who winds it with some ceremony and puts it on its perch. They all wait. After a wowing start the bird sings its old song but with a lopsided rhythm. It is a painful sound

Chancellor There, Excellency, as good as ever! Nearly.

Emperor That is the best that you can do?

Clockmaker It isn't as I would like it but the pins are very worn and it is impossible to renew them. The escapement mechanism has too much play which doesn't help, and one of the sprockets——

Emperor Thank you, there's no need to explain further. I'm sure you have done your best.

Clockmaker There is something else, Excellency. The mechanism has been severely strained. It would be wise to play it no more than once a year otherwise it may break beyond repair.

Emperor I shall remember your advice. No more than once a year.

Clockmaker Good. If you do that, I'm sure it will go like clockwork! Now if you will excuse me I must go and adjust the Imperial Sundial before the weather clouds over.

The Clockmaker goes off ruminating about cogs and sprockets

Emperor There goes a man who still cares whether the sun shines. I wish it was still important to me.

Chancellor Are you ready to see the Imperial Doctor, Excellency?

Emperor Yes. But not if it means all that shouting.

Chancellor Of course, Excellency. (*He goes to the door and calls in a stage whisper*) Call the Imperial Doctor!

Voice (*off, also in a stage whisper*) What?

Chancellor (*shouting as usual*) Call the Imperial Doctor!

The Emperor winces. The Chancellor realizes what he has done

Emperor (*heavily*) Thank you, Chancellor.

The Doctor comes in

Doctor Good-morning, Excellency. How are you today?
Emperor I have taken all of the medicine you prescribed but to no avail. And I'm not surprised since you don't know what is the matter with me.
Doctor (*taking courage*) But I do.
Emperor Then tell me.
Doctor All right. I will tell you the truth if you wish it.
Emperor Go on.
Doctor There is *nothing* wrong with you. You are not ill at all.
Emperor Not ill?
Doctor Not in a way that medicine can cure. You are sick at heart because you are lonely and need true companionship.
Emperor What, has the quack turned philosopher?
Doctor I know that you won't thank me for my advice, but it's the truth.
Emperor So, the Emperor is to hear the truth. I must be even more ill than I thought.
Doctor Why don't you forget your pride and beg the Nightingale to return?
Emperor (*exploding*) Do you dare to question my decisions. The Nightingale is banished. I do not need her and will never ask her to come back.
Chancellor Quite right, Excellency.
Doctor Then I won't be responsible for your health. If you are unwilling to help yourself you will never get well.
Emperor And if you don't get out of this room at once, I'll call the Palace guards and have you thrown into prison! Now, leave me in peace. (*He sinks back and closes his eyes*)
Chancellor His Excellency has no further need of your services.

The Doctor shrugs his shoulders and goes

(*Trying to make the best of things*) I think doctors are very over-rated. What did he mean by saying you need companionship. You always have me for company. (*He peers at the Emperor who seems to be asleep*) Perhaps a sleep will do you good. I'll leave the High Imperial After Dinner Singer beside you. Even if it can't sing it is still very beautiful to look at.

The Housekeeper comes in quietly and moves to the Emperor's bed

Housekeeper And how is our Emperor today?
Chancellor Very ill and getting no better. I try to keep him cheerful but he has little interest in anything and goes weaker, hour by hour. Unless he regains the will to live, I'm afraid there is little hope for him.
Housekeeper It is a great pity for when he was happy he was a good Emperor. I should be very sad to see him die.
Chancellor Let us leave him to sleep.

They go out

Song: The Emperor's Dream

Storyteller (*singing*) May the dreamer dream of evening
                              May the dreamer hear the song

Thrilling through the twilight evening
May the dreaming linger on.

Gold and silver turn to ashes
Power and empires waste away
Priceless is the song he longs for
Life may be the price he'll pay.

May the dreamer dream of evening
May the dreamer hear the song
Thrilling through the twilight evening
May the dreaming linger on.

Mighty prince, he twists and trembles
Dreaming through the nightmare day
Nearby death awaits his victim
Prince's feet are cold as clay.

May the dreamer dream of evening
May the dreamer hear the song
Thrilling through the twilight evening
May the dreaming linger on.

It grows darker. The Emperor stirs in his sleep. He sits up suddenly awaking from a nightmare

Emperor I can scarcely breathe. Who are you who wait in the shadows? I don't want to listen to you. Music, music, bang the drum to keep death away from me. Music, music. Dear little clockwork bird sing, I pray thee, sing! I have given you gold and precious stones, sing for me! (*He falls back, closes his eyes and is still*)

After a moment, Kay Su comes into the room. She moves quietly to the Emperor and looks at him with tenderness

Kay Su Oh, Emperor. Is it true that you are so ill that the Doctor fears for your life? Can nothing save you? (*She moves to the window*) Nightingale, sweet Nightingale! For the last time I ask you, please sing. I know that you will not leave your home in the woods but if you would only sing I am sure you could awaken the Emperor. (*To the audience*) Will you help me to call her? All together, but quietly ... we don't want to frighten her. Nightingale ... Nightingale ...

A pause then the Nightingale sings. Kay Su listens overjoyed. After a moment the Emperor opens is eyes

Oh, thank you. You have made me so happy!
Emperor Kay Su!

Kay Su turns and for a moment wonders if she should run away

What are you afraid of me? Come here, child, and tell me that I am forgiven.

She goes to him and takes his hand

I banished the Nightingale from my realm and yet she has sung away the face of death and brought me back to my happier self. How can I reward her?

The Nightingale sings

Kay Su The Nightingale says that she saw tears in your eyes when she sang for you the first time and will never forget them.

Emperor Tell her that she shall stay with me always, she shall sing only when it pleases her and that I will break the clockwork bird into a thousand pieces.

Kay Su Oh no, you mustn't do that. It has done what it could. The Nightingale will never return to the Palace but she will live in the woods and sit in the branches close to your window in the evening and sing to you of all the things she sees in the world.

Emperor What a fool I have been! That will not be possible.

Kay Su Why?

Emperor There will be no place for the Nightingale. I ordered the Architect to cut down all the trees in the wood to make way for my new garden. There is nowhere for her to live now.

Kay Su Don't worry. Your woods have been spared. The Architect could not bring himself to destroy the trees even though it meant disobeying your orders.

Emperor Then he has my undying gratitude. He has turned out to be a wiser man than me. How can I ever repay him?

Kay Su I think I can tell you.

Emperor Yes?

Kay Su I know what would please him most. There is a heap of bricks and stones ...

Emperor (*taking up the story*) ... left over from when the kitchen was rebuilt. And he would like to use them to make new quarters for the palace servants!

Kay Su That's right!

Emperor Oh well, perhaps he'd better. He has shown himself wise in other things—perhaps this is an act of wisdom too. You can call him now if you like.

Kay Su opens the door

The Architect who has been listening at the keyhole falls into the room

Architect No need, Excellency. I just happened to be passing and couldn't help overhearing your conversation.

Emperor (*with a smile*) You are fortunate. Listeners don't usually hear good of themselves.

Architect I'm sure that your people will be very pleased when I tell them the news. (*He goes to Kay Su and holds her hand*) Thank you, Kay Su.

Emperor And there's something else you can tell them.
Architect Yes?
Emperor That from today the Imperial Gardens will be open to everybody.
I see now the folly of keeping beautiful things to myself.
Kay Su Excellency ...
Emperor I'm afraid I can't offer you your old job as the Nightingale no
longer needs a keeper. But you may wear the golden kimono again if it
pleases you.
Kay Su I don't think it would be very suitable for what I have in mind.
Emperor And that is?
Kay Su I would like to help the Architect to build the new houses for your
servants.
Emperor (*with a twinkle*) That seems a good idea. I expect you will be
needing a place for yourselves soon.

The Architect looks at Kay Su and nods with a smile

Let us go and look at the site together. (*He goes to the door and calls*)
Chancellor! I think I know somebody who's in for a big surprise!
Chancellor (*appearing at the doorway*) Why, Excellency you're better.
Emperor I think I am, thanks to Kay Su and the Nightingale. Chancellor,
fetch my doctor.

The Chancellor is about to call him but thinks better of it

Chancellor Yes, Excellency.

The Chancellor goes off to find him

The Clockmaker hurries in

Clockmaker I am very pleased to hear that you are recovered, Excellency.
Er ... now that the true Nightingale has returned, perhaps you will
permit me to look after the mechanical bird. It will keep me company and
I'll handle it with great care.
Emperor All right, old tick-tock.

The Housekeeper comes in

Housekeeper Excellency, I'm so pleased to see you well again.
Emperor Thank you.

The Doctor enters followed by the Chancellor

Doctor You sent for me, Excellency.
Emperor Yes, your honesty put me in a rage but now I see that it was the
best medicine you could have given me. I hope you will forgive my
outburst and return to the Palace.
Doctor Of course, Excellency.
Emperor Thank you. And now, Kay Su and my Architect and I are going
into the garden to look at the site of the new servants' quarters and to
listen to the song of the Nightingale. You are all welcome to come with us.
And Chancellor ...
Chancellor Yes, Excellency.

Emperor You may tell the Imperial Undertaker that I won't be requiring his services today after all!

The Emperor follows the Architect and Kay Su into the garden and the others follow in procession

The Nightingale sings and goes on singing as——

—the CURTAIN *falls*

FURNITURE AND PROPERTY LIST

Only essential items are listed. Further dressing may be added at the director's discretion

ACT I

SCENE 1

On stage: PALACE AREA
Throne
Small table. *On it:* books, etc.
WOOD AREA
Trees

Off stage: Plans (**Architect**)

SCENE 2

On stage: As before

Personal: **Housekeeper:** duster

SCENE 3

Strike: Garden plan from throne

Off stage: Beautifully bound illustrated book (**Chancellor**)
Striped poles, ropes, surveying equipment (**Architect**)

Personal: **Chancellor:** watch

SCENE 4

Off stage: Striped pole, ropes, surveying equipment (**Architect**)

Personal: **Kay Su:** posy of flowers

SCENE 5

On stage: As before

Off stage: Striped pole, ropes, surveying equipment (**Architect**)

Personal: **Chancellor:** small wicker basket
Clockmaker: pocket watch (worn throughout)

SCENE 6

On stage: Nightingale in tree

SCENE 7

On stage: As before

Off stage: Small golden cage containing Nightingale, on red velvet cushion **(Page)**
Golden kimono **(Page)**

ACT II

SCENE 1

On stage: As before

Off stage: Package containing clockwork Nightingale (practical) covered with precious stones **(Architect)**
Nightingale's cage

SCENE 2

On stage: As before

SCENE 3

On stage: As before

Off stage: Ropes, poles etc. **(Architect)**

SCENE 4

On stage: As before

Personal: **Doctor:** stethoscope, paper, pen

SCENE 5

On stage: As before

SCENE 6

Set: Footstool in front of throne

Off stage: Repaired clockwork Nightingale **(Clockmaker)**

LIGHTING PLOT

Property fittings required: nil.

Composite set: a palace and a wood. The same throughout

ACT I

To open: General lighting on throne room

Cue 1	**Chancellor:** "I'm certain nobody else has!" *Cross fade to wood area*	(Page 10)
Cue 2	**Architect:** "Hurry please, we haven't much time ..." *Cross fade to palace area*	(Page 12)
Cue 3	**Clockmaker:** "... tick, tock, tick, tock ..." *Cross fade to wood area*	(Page 14)
Cue 4	**Chancellor:** "Now you couldn't have fairer than that ..." *Cross fade to palace area*	(Page 15)

ACT II

To open: General lighting on throne room

Cue 5	As "Sprockets and Ratchets" finishes *Cross fade to palace area*	(Page 22)
Cue 6	**Housekeeper:** "Even if it's only in her dreams ..." *Cross fade to wood area*	(Page 23)
Cue 7	**Architect:** "... my heart isn't in it I suppose ..." *Cross fade to throne room*	(Page 24)
Cue 8	**Emperor:** "No wonder I don't feel well." *Cross fade to wood area*	(Page 28)
Cue 9	As "Who Would Be A Doctor" finishes *Cross fade to throne room*	(Page 30)
Cue 10	As "The Emperor's Dream" finishes *Dim lighting*	(Page 33)
Cue 11	As **Kay Su** enters *Increase lighting*	(Page 33)

EFFECTS PLOT

ACT I

ACT II

IF YOU COULD CLIMB INSIDE MY HEAD

have to think of some - thing else in - stead. We'll put
ac - tors in the scenes, And they'll dra-ma-tise the dreams Since
you can't climb in - side my head. In the
far a - way time of 'once - u - pon - a - time' In a
once - u - pon - a - far - a - way land.

EVERYTHING IN THE EMPEROR'S GARDEN

GREY BIRD

No-thing much to look at lit-tle grey bird lit - tle
grey bird, I'm a grey bird too Grey bird grey
bird, Lit-tle grey bird, I'm a grey bird too. How I
wish that I could sing How I wish that I had wings I would
fly fly a - way and be like you FINE. Not for
me the spring - time blos - som Not for
fro - zen roots of win - ter I'm un-
me the trees in au - tumn Not for
no - ticed and for - got - ten. How I
me the sum - mer sky in sun - shine
Like the wish that I could be like you.
D.C. AL FINE.

And the sto - ry spin - ning in my head Has on - ly
half been told, The ac - tors have the de - tails Which they'll
ve - ry soon un - fold. The Arch - i - tect, the Chan-
- cel - lor, The Em - per - or and all Are
stand - ing in the wings Where they're wait-ing for the
CHORUS.
call. And when the Night - in - gale sings I
know that ev - ery - bo - dy sings. And when ev - ery -
bo - dy sings I know what hap - pi - ness it brings So,
sing lit-tle Night - in - gale, Sing lit - tle Night-in-gale,
Sing lit - tle Night - in - gale, Sing.

WHEN THE NIGHTINGALE SINGS

SPROCKETS AND RATCHETS

WHO WOULD BE A DOCTOR

Who Would Be A Doctor

He'll find no cure in tablets
In potions or in pills
Everybody knows but him
The medicine for his ills.

Dearie me, dearie me,
Oh, dear, dearie me!
Everybody knows but him
The medicine for his ills.

But if our Doctor tells him
It may land him in a mess
He might be banished from the kingdom
Or something even worse!

Dearie me, dearie me,
Oh, dear, dearie me!
He might be banished from the kingdom
Or something even worse!

He could even have his head chopped off
Or be strung up from a tree
I can't tell you what night happen
You'll just have to wait and see.

Dearie me, dearie me,
Oh, dear, dearie me!
I can't tell you what might happen
You'll just have to wait and see.

THE EMPEROR'S DREAM
May the dream - er dream of eve - ning
May the dream - er hear the song
Thrill - ing through the twi - light eve - ning
May the dream - ing lin - ger on.
1.Gold and sil - ver turn to ash - es
2.Might - y prince, he twists and trem - bles
Power and em - pires waste a - way
Dream - ing through the night - mare day
Price - less is the song he longs for
Near - by death a - waits his vic - tim
Life may be the price he'll pay.
Prin - ce's feet are cold as clay.
May the dream - ing lin - ger on.